KINGFISHER KNOWLEDGE

THE MIDDLE EAST

▶ Camels cross trackless sand
dunes in the United Arab Emirates.

THE MIDDLE
EAST

Philip Steele

Foreword by
Paul Adams

KINGFISHER

Senior editor: Catherine Brereton
Designer: Rebecca Painter
Consultant: Dr Anthony Gorman, School of
Oriental and African Studies, University of London
Picture research manager: Cee Weston-Baker
Senior production controller: Lindsey Scott
DTP co-ordinator: Catherine Hibbert
Indexer: Diana Le Core

KINGFISHER

Kingfisher Publications Plc, New Penderel House,
283–288 High Holborn, London WC1V 7HZ
www.kingfisherpub.com

First published by Kingfisher Publications Plc 2006
10 9 8 7 6 5 4 3 2 1

1TR/0706/TWP/MA(MA)/130ENSOMA/F

ISBN-10: 0 7534 1323 X
ISBN-13: 978 0 7534 1323 4

Printed in Singapore

915.6

GO FURTHER...
INFORMATION PANEL KEY:

websites and
further reading

career paths

places to visit

Contents

CHAPTER 2
MODERN NATIONS   29

NOTE TO READERS
The website addresses listed in this book are correct at the time of going to print. However, due to the ever-changing nature of the internet, website addresses and content can change. Websites can contain links that are unsuitable for children. The publisher cannot be held responsible for changes in website addresses or content, or for information obtained through third-party websites. We strongly advise that internet searches should be supervised by an adult.

▼ An oil refinery in Shaybah, Saudi Arabia, sits surrounded by desert. Oil is the most important industry in the Middle East.

Foreword

What is it about the Middle East? It never seems to be out of the news for long. It is a collection of countries which throws up more than its fair share of headlines, a region of deserts and rocky hillsides which preoccupies world leaders more than almost anywhere else, and sometimes threatens global stability.

I grew up with the Middle East. I was born in Lebanon and my father, a journalist like me, devoted most of his adult life to the region and its conflicts. I've found myself going back there again and again. For all its difficulties, it is a compelling part of the world. At the BBC, we often ask ourselves how we can bring this complicated region to life for our viewers and listeners. This book does a wonderful job.

There are many great cities here: Cairo, teeming with life; Damascus and Sana, full of oriental colour; Istanbul, a rich meeting point of cultures and continents. But it's perhaps Jerusalem that offers the key to the rest of the world's obsession with the Middle East. Sitting in the centre of the region, looking west and east, it's a cauldron of history, religion and politics. Living there, I often used to think that Jerusalem was cursed by being *too* important to too many people. Jews, Christians and Muslims compete for holy space inside the walls of the old city. Israelis and Palestinians both claim it as their capital. As you walk around, the streets seem to speak of dramatic events down the ages: Jewish revolts against Roman rule, battles between Arabs and crusaders, and, in recent years, a long list of bloody episodes involving Israelis and Palestinians.

Once, trapped between demonstrating Palestinians and Israeli paramilitary police, I ducked behind one of the heavy wooden doors that lead on to the Muslim Noble Sanctuary (known by Jews as the Temple Mount) as a plastic baton round hurtled towards me. But in doing so, I unwittingly used an entrance barred to foreign visitors, and found myself in the confusion and noise of a full-scale riot. Linger in Jerusalem for any length of time and you'll find yourself caught up in one of this ancient city's many struggles.

Of course, there are those who look for other reasons for our obsession with the Middle East. On page 25, you'll see that more than 60 per cent of the world's proven oil reserves lie under the sands of the region. We're using it up fast, but the politics and economics of oil will be with us for decades to come. When foreign troops marched into Iraq in 2003, securing that country's vast and lucrative oil fields was an important task. Some people said oil, and not Saddam Hussein's elusive 'weapons of mass destruction', was the reason the USA, Britain and others went to war in the first place, although both governments denied this.

As you can see, it's easy to portray the Middle East as a region of conflict and division. But it's also the cradle of civilization, where farming and writing first developed. It's littered with magnificent remains, including the Nabatean city of Petra, in modern-day Jordan, which fans of Indiana Jones will recognize from *The Last Crusade*.

As the 2003 Iraq war drew to an end, talks about the country's political future took place under the shadow of another monument: the 4,000-year-old ziggurat of Ur. It was a reminder, to all those present, of this troubled region's glorious past.

Whether it's today's world events or the earliest achievements of civilization that capture your imagination, why don't you spend a little time exploring this remarkable part of the world!

Paul Adams

Paul Adams, BBC Diplomatic Correspondent and former Middle East Correspondent

CHAPTER 1

People and places

The Middle East is a diverse and fascinating region, often in the news, and what happens in the Middle East is important to the whole world. In its broad river valleys, humans first learned to farm. It was here that people first built cities and created great empires, governed by the rule of law. Out of these deserts, oases and valleys came religious beliefs that still guide the lives of millions of people around the world. The region's history has always been stormy. In modern times the discovery of oil has brought wealth to some, but has also made powerful nations want to gain control over the region. Too often the news from the Middle East has been of war, but it should not be forgotten that the peoples of the Middle East have a rich culture, a tradition of friendship and a great desire for peace with justice.

Rugs are rolled out for morning prayers at Mecca, Islam's holiest city, in Saudi Arabia.

▲ Olive groves and wheat fields cover the chalky hills of northern Syria, near the Turkish border. In many Middle Eastern countries, the lack of fertile land, and insufficient rainfall, allow only limited opportunities for farming.

▲ Israeli children celebrate the feast of Purim with gifts of food and parades. Most of the festivals celebrated in the Middle East are rooted in the region's history or religious beliefs. Purim recalls the story of Queen Esther in ancient Persia (modern-day Iran).

Map labels:
Black Sea
Istanbul
Ankara
ANATOLIA
TURKEY
Taurus Mountains
Aleppo
LEBANON
SYRI
Palestinian Territories
CYPRUS
Beirut
Damascus
Mediterranean Sea
ISRAEL
Tel Aviv
Amman
JORDA
Jerusalem
Alexandria
Cairo
Petra
Pyramids at Giza
EGYPT
Nile
Red Sea
Mecca

Where in the world?

We often hear newsreaders or politicians talking about the 'Middle East'. It is a useful name describing the lands of southwest Asia and northeast Africa, but it is not a very precise term. Some people might leave out African countries, or Turkey or Afghanistan, others might include more countries in north Africa or central Asia. In the past, many other names have been used to describe parts of the region, such as Asia Minor, Mesopotamia, the Near East, the Holy Land or the Levant. The Middle East we explore in this book consists of Turkey, Syria, Lebanon, Israel and the Palestinian Territories, Egypt, Jordan, Saudi Arabia, Yemen, Oman, the Gulf states, Iraq, Iran and Afghanistan.

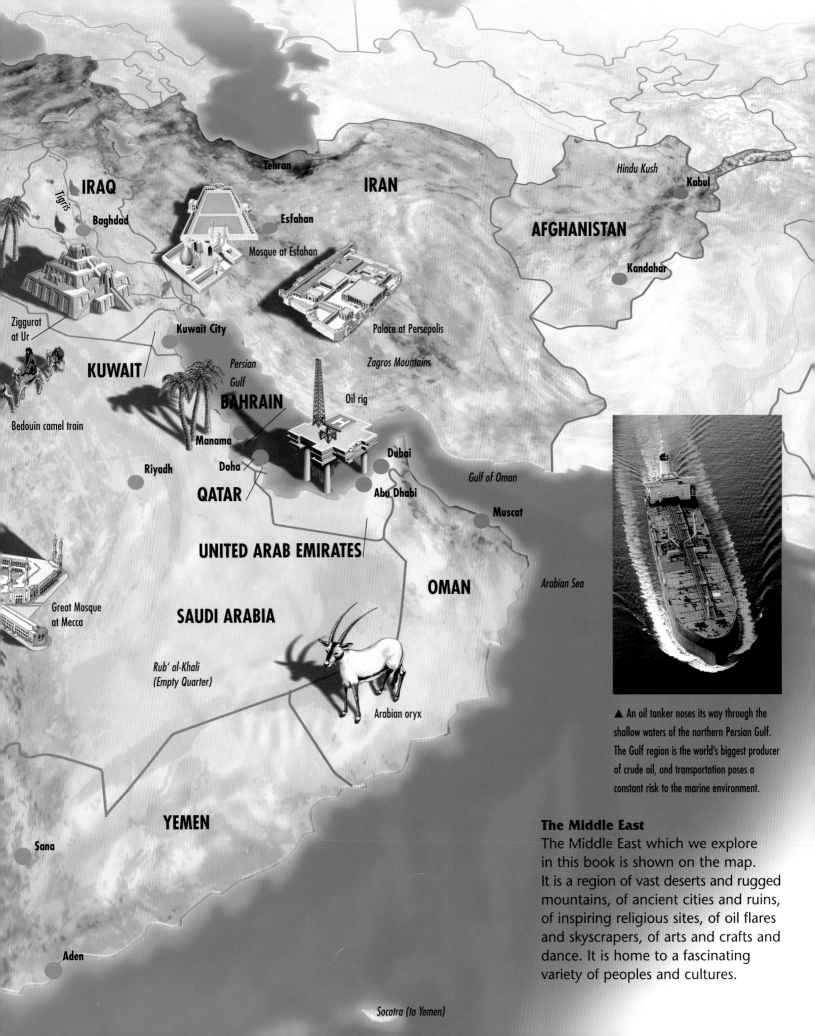

IRAQ

Tigris

Baghdad

Ziggurat
at Ur

Bedouin camel train

KUWAIT

Kuwait City

Tehran

Esfahan

Mosque at Esfahan

IRAN

Hindu Kush

Kabul

AFGHANISTAN

Kandahar

Palace at Persepolis

Zagros Mountains

Persian
Gulf

BAHRAIN

Manama

Riyadh

Doha

QATAR

Oil rig

Dubai

Abu Dhabi

Gulf of Oman

Muscat

UNITED ARAB EMIRATES

OMAN

Arabian Sea

Great Mosque
at Mecca

SAUDI ARABIA

Rub' al-Khali
(Empty Quarter)

Arabian oryx

YEMEN

Sana

Aden

Socotra (to Yemen)

▲ An oil tanker noses its way through the
shallow waters of the northern Persian Gulf.
The Gulf region is the world's biggest producer
of crude oil, and transportation poses a
constant risk to the marine environment.

The Middle East
The Middle East which we explore
in this book is shown on the map.
It is a region of vast deserts and rugged
mountains, of ancient cities and ruins,
of inspiring religious sites, of oil flares
and skyscrapers, of arts and crafts and
dance. It is home to a fascinating
variety of peoples and cultures.

Land and climate

The lands of the Middle East cover an area of over 9.6 million km². Across this vast region are barren deserts made up of shifting sand dunes, gravel, rocks and shimmering salt flats. Here too are dusty, windswept plains and snow-capped mountains, long rivers and fertile valleys, wetlands, lake shores and tropical coasts with coral reefs. Many of these environments are fragile and under threat.

Across the deserts

The Arabian Desert is the third largest in the world. From here, deserts stretch northwards to Syria, and westwards across Egypt to the Sahara. Three great rivers cross these arid lands. The Tigris and Euphrates rise in Turkey and flow southwards through Iraq to the Gulf. The Nile flows northwards across Egypt into the Mediterranean Sea. Mountains ring Turkey's Anatolian plateau and also rise in western and northern Iran. Beyond the bleak deserts of eastern Iran are Afghanistan's dizzying gorges and rock-strewn river valleys.

◀ Coral reefs form a wondrous underwater world in the Red Sea. This narrow sea is part of a deep crack in the earth's crust, known as the Great Rift Valley. The rift continues northwards along the low-lying Jordan valley and southwards through Africa.

▶ Two Egyptian boys clamber up a date palm at an oasis, a desert location where there is a source of water. With tough fronds and slender trunks, date palms survive well in very hot, dry climates. Several Middle Eastern countries are known for their date harvests (see page 24). However, they need plenty of water to thrive and bear fruit.

▼ The Arabian oryx is an endangered species. This beautiful desert antelope was hunted to the verge of extinction by the 1970s. However, it was bred in captivity and reintroduced into Jordan, Oman, Saudi Arabia, Bahrain and Israel.

Temperature extremes

Mediterranean coasts have mild, moist winters and warm summers. Further from the sea, the climate is continental, with very hot summers and cold winters, especially icy in the mountains. Deserts experience extremes of temperature. In Saudi Arabia's Rub' al-Khali desert (the 'Empty Quarter'), a blistering daytime temperature of 60°C can drop to freezing point overnight. Here, there can be no rainfall for years on end.

The natural world

Famous plants of the Middle East include the cedar trees of Lebanon, the wild tulips of Turkey and Jordan, and the walnut trees of Iran and Afghanistan. Native animals include wild goats, desert foxes and small rodents such as jerboas. The natural environment has been affected by irrigation and draining, by over-grazing, deforestation, warfare and pollution from the oil industry.

People and languages

Over 340 million people live in the countries described in this book. Many of them share similar living conditions, housing, food or dress. However, there are also many differences in their origins, in their languages and dialects, their customs and their religious beliefs. National borders do not always match these groupings. For example, Kurds are to be found living in Turkey, Syria, Iraq and Iran.

Ways of living

In the Middle East there are both ultra-modern cities and regions where people's lives have changed little since ancient times. There are desert nomads, who live in tents and move from one oasis to the next with their flocks. There are farming villages in areas of fertile countryside. Concrete and glass apartment blocks, hotels and offices tower over more modern cities. Many country people move to the cities in search of work.

▼ A rich patchwork of cultures and peoples extends across the Middle East. Dress may be modern or traditional, often reflecting the history or religious practices of an ethnic group. Some types of dress were first used because they protected people from heat or dust storms in the desert.

Pashtun elder, Afghanistan

young woman, Iraq

Orthodox Jew, Israel

schoolboy, Yemen

Marsh Arab, Iraq

صباح الخير

בקר טוב

Günaydın

bayaanii baash

▲ Alphabets were a Middle Eastern invention, and these four alphabets are among those used in the region today. This is the phrase 'good morning' in (from top) Arabic, Hebrew, Turkish and Kurdish. The flowing lines of Arabic make it ideal for calligraphy, or decorative writing, which is practised as a fine art.

Peoples and cultures

People who share a common descent, culture or language form an ethnic group. They may or may not share the same nationality. The Arabs form the largest ethnic group in the Middle East. Their original homeland is the whole Arabian peninsula and they are also found across Jordan, Iraq, Syria, Lebanon, the Palestinian Territories, Israel and North Africa. Other major ethnic groups in the Middle East include Persians, Kurds, Turks and Jews.

Language groups

People in the Middle East speak a wide variety of languages. The Semitic language group includes the Arabic language, which has many dialects, as well as Hebrew, one of the main languages of Israel. The Turkic group includes Turkish, Azeri, Turkmen, Uzbek and Tajik. The vast Indo-European language group, which extends from Western Europe to India, takes in Greek, Kurdish, Farsi, Dari and Pashto.

Persian woman, Iran

woman in traditional dress, Saudi Arabia

Arab family, Bahrain

Holy lands

Three of the world's great religions were born in the Middle East – Judaism, Christianity and Islam. In history, there have been periods of both peace and war between followers of these religions, but the three faiths actually have much in common. At the centre of all of them is a belief in one God. The Middle East is home to some other religions as well. The oldest of these is probably Zoroastrianism.

Judaism

Judaism is the religion of the Jews. They believe that in ancient times they were chosen by God as his favoured people, and promised the land of Canaan (later known as Palestine or Israel). Jews believe that God revealed his Law or Torah to Moses. Jews worship at a synagogue ('meeting place'). Their holy day or Sabbath lasts from sunset on Friday to sunset on Saturday. The number of Jews in the Middle East has been estimated at just over 5 million.

▲ Jews pray at dawn, at Jerusalem's Western Wall. They are commemorating the destruction of their Temple, which took place in 586BCE and again in 70CE. They carry the Torah, the scriptures that they believe contain the Law of God as revealed to Moses.

◄ Jesus Christ died in Jerusalem in about 30CE. His cross became a symbol of the Christian faith. This spread rapidly to other lands, such as Egypt, where there has been a Christian community for over 1,900 years. Worldwide, Christians may now number over 2.1 billion.

Christianity

Christians live in many parts of the Middle East. They respect the ancient Jewish scriptures, which they call the Old Testament. The rest of their holy book, the Bible, is made up of the New Testament. This declares that Jesus Christ, a Jew born over 2,000 years ago in Bethlehem, was the Son of God. Having been crucified (executed on a cross), they believe he rose from the dead and ascended into heaven. Various branches of the faith developed over the ages. The Christian holy day is Sunday, when the faithful gather to pray and worship in churches.

► Egyptian Muslims are called to prayer by this muezzin (proclaimer) at the Blue Mosque in Cairo, Egypt. Islam has spread around the world from Arabia and now has about 1.3 billion followers.

▼ The pilgrimage to Mecca in Saudi Arabia, called the *hajj*, is a sacred duty for every Muslim capable of the journey. Rituals are performed at Islam's holiest sites. The *tawaf* involves walking around the *Ka`ba*, the black monument seen in the centre of this scene.

Islam

Islam means 'submission' to the will of God. Its followers, Muslims, make up by far the largest religious group in the Middle East. The Koran is their holy scripture, their place of worship is the mosque and their holy day is Friday. They believe that Abraham, Moses and Jesus were prophets, but that Muhammad, an Arab from Mecca born in about 570CE, was the last and greatest of the prophets and the Messenger of God. Muslims must declare their faith, pray five times a day, give alms, fast during the month of Ramadan and go on pilgrimage.

Islam has two main branches: Sunni and Shi'a. Sunnis believe that their leaders, caliphs, are simply guardians of the Koran, while Shi'ites believe their leaders, called imams, can reinterpret its meaning.

▼ Each year Zoroastrian pilgrims visit the temple of Chakchak, near Yazd, Iran. They light candles, because fire is a sacred symbol of their faith. The Zoroastrian religion is based upon the teachings of Zoroaster, who may have lived in Persia (Iran) about 3,000 years ago.

Where civilization began

Ancient peoples of the Middle East were probably the first in the world to domesticate animals and grow crops. They were the first to build walled towns and great cities, where the first civilizations could flourish, with governments and laws. It was here that hours were first counted as 60 minutes. It was here, too, that the wheel was invented, that writing was first used, that bronze and iron were first worked by metal smiths, and glass was first made. All these developments took place over thousands of years.

▲ The region revived as a centre of civilization in the Middle Ages. Scholarship, poetry and architecture thrived. This illustration is from the *Maqamat* (Assemblies) of al-Hariri and was produced in about 1100CE. It shows a library at Basra, in Iraq.

▲ This wall painting from about 1300BCE shows an Egyptian farmer ploughing with oxen on the banks of the river Nile. The soil was fertile, thanks to the layers of mud left behind by the floods each year. The need to calculate the seasons for sowing and harvest led to the development of the first calendars.

Farmers, smiths and builders

Farming developed from about 8000BCE in the Fertile Crescent, a region stretching westwards from Mesopotamia (modern-day Iraq), the land between the rivers Tigris and Euphrates. With an assured supply of food, farmers could settle in one place and trade any extra grain for other goods. As a result, towns grew up. By the third millennium BCE, huge monuments were being built. The pyramids of Egypt were royal tombs, while the ziggurats of Mesopotamia were massive temple platforms. Urban populations developed new technologies. Bronze was used widely in the region from about 3200BCE. Ironworking began in Anatolia (Turkey) in about 1300BCE.

royal procession accompanied by attendants and musicians

▲ The ziggurat at Ur was a huge mountain made of brick, built in about 2100BCE. It was dedicated to Nanna, the moon-god, who was believed to live on the summit with his wife Nin-Gal. Religious ceremonies and sacrifices were held in the temple, and royal processions sometimes took place outside the temple.

Libraries and scholars

The ruins of splendid ancient cities such as Persepolis can still be seen in Iran. They date from the first Persian empire, founded in 550BCE. The Persians were conquered by Greeks, who brought their own graceful styles of sculpture and architecture into western Asia. The city of Alexandria, founded by Alexander the Great in Egypt, became famous for its great library, its scholars and geographers.

Medieval civilizations

In the Middle Ages, Greek, Roman and Asian cultures mingled in the Byzantine empire, with its law courts, palaces and beautiful religious buildings. This period, too, saw a golden age of Islamic civilization. Arabs and Persians were great astronomers, mathematicians, doctors, musicians and poets. Many words in the English language, such as 'algebra' and 'lute', are Arabic in origin.

sailing boats on Euphrates

religious ceremony taking place in the Temple of Nanna

ziggurat (step-sided pyramid)

sheep at market

wheeled chariot

▶ People brought animals and goods to trade in the city's market. Writing using picture symbols began in Mesopotamia in about 7000BCE and was first used as a way of recording sales. By about 3400BCE wedge-shaped ('cuneiform') marks pressed into clay were used as a script. Alphabets with letters date back to at least 1500BCE.

The march of empires

The history of the Middle East is characterized by armies on the march and battles. It is a history of proud rulers who built great cities, temples and palaces. Today, their gigantic statues and pillars of stone lie ruined, but they still impress us. The kingdom of ancient Egypt was founded in about 3000BCE, when Upper and Lower Egypt were united. The world's first empire (a country that rules over lands it has conquered), dates from about 2300BCE. It was created when Akkadians conquered the Sumerians. Some peoples sought economic power rather than empires. The Phoenicians, seafarers from the eastern Mediterranean, traded as far away as the British Isles.

Peoples of the ancient world

The city of Babylon, in Mesopotamia, was twice capital of a powerful empire. The first empire saw the world's earliest known legal code inscribed on stone, during the reign of Hammurabi (from 1792 to about 1750BCE). In the second Babylonian empire (625–538BCE), King Nebuchadnezzar II rebuilt the city with magnificent streets and a great temple and palace, and planted the palace's leafy terraces known as the Hanging Gardens of Babylon. The first Babylonians battled with the Hittites. This warlike people from Anatolia were the first to master the use of iron. The Assyrians governed much of the Middle East in the 9th century BCE and were also famed as ruthless warriors, masters of the war chariot.

◀ This bronze head was made some time in the third millennium BCE. It represents an Akkadian ruler, perhaps the great Sargon. He founded the world's first great empire, which stretched from the Gulf to the eastern Mediterranean. It may, however, represent a later ruler, Naram-Sin, who conquered the inhabitants of the Zagros mountains.

► The eighth gate of the city of Babylon was dedicated to the goddess Ishtar and faced with glazed blue tiles decorated with bulls and dragons. It was built for Nebuchadnezzar II, who ruled from 605 to 562BCE.

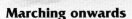

Marching onwards

The first Persian empire (c. 550–330BCE) ruled lands from Egypt to Central Asia. When King Xerxes advanced against Greece in 480BCE, 47 different nationalities marched in his army. Even this great empire was conquered, in 331BCE, by a Greek force under Alexander the Great. Later, Roman soldiers marched east, reaching Palestine in the 60s BCE.

The last great empires

Medieval armies included the Arabs in the 7th century CE, holy warriors of Islam, and Christian crusaders from Europe in the 11th. Other fierce invaders rode in from the east, such as the Seljuk and Ottoman Turks. In 1206, a Mongol warlord declared himself 'ruler of the world' – Genghis Khan. A new Persian empire reached its peak about 400 years ago, and the Ottoman empire lasted until 1922, but by then the age of large Middle Eastern empires was drawing to a close.

▲ The Ottoman empire was founded in 1299 and from 1453 had its capital at Constantinople (now Istanbul). This picture shows its army fighting against the Hungarians in Europe, in 1566. Ottoman power was at its height at this time.

▲ The Romans often met fierce resistance during their occupation of the Middle East in the 1st century BCE and 1st and 2nd centuries CE. They suppressed a major Jewish rebellion in 70CE and sacked Jerusalem. Sacred treasures looted from its temple were paraded through Rome, as shown by this carving.

Arts and culture

The Sumerians invented the lyre, a stringed instrument, as early as 3200BCE. Their craftsmen dazzled with gold, bronze, pearls, shell and the brilliant blue stone called lapis lazuli. Sumerians wrote the first literature, telling wonderful tales about Gilgamesh, the legendary king of Uruk. The ancient Egyptians too produced lively wall paintings, harps and jewellery. Beautiful objects were left in tombs for dead rulers to take with them to the next world. The Middle East continued to produce marvellous arts and crafts for thousands of years, such as silk and satin textiles, silver, pottery, Persian and Turkish carpets.

▲ This elaborately worked casket is a reliquary, designed to hold sacred Christian relics in the 9th or 10th century CE. It was made in the Byzantine empire, whose capital was at Constantinople (Istanbul).

Another kind of music

The Arabian musical tradition has had a wide influence across the Middle East. While European classical music has eight notes and five half-tones in a scale, the Arabian form has up to 24 notes in a scale, with quarter tones. It is not based on harmony, and uses complex rhythms. Traditional eastern instruments include the oud (ancestor of the lute), bowed string instruments, wind instruments and hand drums.

◄ Western views of the Middle East have been shaped by the *Tales from the 1,001 Nights*, a collection of Arabian, Persian and Indian folk stories. They were first written down in Arabic in about 850CE. They feature characters that have become well known worldwide, such as Sindbad, Ali Baba and Aladdin.

► Richly patterned carpets are dried on a cliff in Iran. Carpet-making has a history of at least 2,500 years and has become an art in its own right.

◄ Middle Eastern artists explore modern themes as well as more traditional ones. This film examines life in Afghanistan in 2004. It was directed by a young Iranian woman called Samira Makhmalbaf and is called *Panj é Asr* ('Five in the Afternoon').

Poetry and performance

Middle Eastern music often involves the recital of stories and verse. Persia (now Iran) has a great history of poetry inspired both by human love and by Sufism, a mystical form of Islam. Sufis seek direct experience of God through music, dance or meditation. Acting or drama has not traditionally been common in the Middle East, but Turkey has long been famous for its clever shadow puppets, used to act out folk tales in popular shows.

Pictures and patterns

The art of the medieval period included the sacred Christian paintings or 'icons' of the Byzantine empire, as well as Persian miniature paintings of court life and everyday scenes of Baghdad life. Although the human figure does feature in some Islamic art it is less common than in western art, and mosques were decorated with beautifully elaborate writing (calligraphy) in the Arabic script, or intricate patterns of flowers. Beautiful abstract designs can also be seen in oriental carpets, embroidery, intricate woodworking, filigree (fine metal), tile and enamel work.

Merchants and bazaars

Middle Eastern trade is as old as the first towns. Early potters, weavers and metalworkers exchanged goods to make a living. Later, the Phoenicians traded in metal ores, animal hides and textile dyes. In about 630BCE, the world's first metal coins were issued in what is now Turkey. Trading routes grew up across deserts, mountains and oceans. As goods flowed along these routes, so too did ideas, new religions, crafts and technologies. Trade funded the great cities and empires of history.

Spices and silk

One centre of trade in ancient times was the Red Sea coast. Ancient Egyptians, Axumites and Edomites all traded in incense, myrrh, gold and ivory. Spices from India and Southeast Asia passed through Arabian cities such as Petra and Damascus. Another important trading network from about 200BCE was the Silk Road. Goods including bales of silk, bricks of tea, precious stones and porcelain were relayed from China to the Mediterranean through Central Asia, Persia and Syria.

▲ Petra, in Jordan, was a desert city, with its buildings cut out of pink sandstone cliffs. It reached the height of its prosperity in the first century CE, when it profited from the caravans bringing eastern spices. Its rulers were an Arab people, known as Nabataeans.

Caravans and caravanserai

Business along the Silk Road peaked in the 9th century CE. Merchants travelled together in convoys called caravans. Their goods were relayed by strings of camels or packhorses, across desolate deserts and mountain passes. The merchandise was sold on from one town to the next. In the towns were stopping places called caravanserai, where merchants could sleep, rest and store their goods.

▲ A camel caravan crosses the desert. The dromedary or one-humped camel is native to Arabia. It can carry heavy loads for at least 40km a day and can travel for six days without water. Desert traders travelled from one oasis to another.

In the market

Common Middle Eastern words for 'market' include souk and bazaar. Markets have always been at the heart of everyday life in the Middle East. Many were covered markets, with small shops and tea rooms opening on to a maze of alleys. The tailors would all be on one street, the copper smiths on another, the carpet sellers on another... Haggling over prices was the way to do business.

▲ The Arabs invented the triangular or 'lateen' sail, seen here off the coast of Zanzibar on a mashua or small sailing boat. This East African island was ruled by Omani sultans from 1698.

Sailing with the monsoons

The seasonal winds called monsoons, which sweep across the Indian Ocean, took large wooden merchant ships called dhows from the Red Sea and the Gulf to India and Southeast Asia. In the Middle Ages, Arab and Persian merchants settled around the coasts and islands of East Africa, where their culture merged with that of the local peoples to form the Swahili civilization.

▲ An array of delicious dates goes on sale in Istanbul's Kapali Çarsi or 'covered bazaar'. This market dates back to the year 1461 CE. It includes thousands of shops, cafes, workshops, fountains and mosques. Business is generally carried out over glasses of black tea.

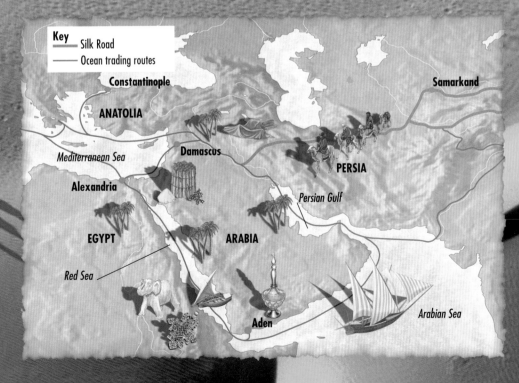

▶ Trade with East, Central and Southeast Asia followed well-established routes by land and sea for over a thousand years. Goods were traded on from one town or port to the next before reaching the Middle East or continuing westwards to Europe.

Key
— Silk Road
— Ocean trading routes

Constantinople

Samarkand

ANATOLIA

Mediterranean Sea

Damascus

PERSIA

Alexandria

Persian Gulf

EGYPT

ARABIA

Red Sea

Aden

Arabian Sea

Resources and work

The two most precious resources in the Middle East are cool, fresh water and sticky black oil. In a region of hot deserts, water means survival. It quenches thirst, irrigates crops and keeps pastures green. In a world desperate for fuel, the Middle East's rich reserves of oil bring wealth and employment to dusty lands with few other natural advantages.

▲ A handful of dates, from Saudi Arabia. Other major date growers are Iraq, Iran and Egypt. Date palms thrive in arid lands and have been cultivated in the Middle East for at least 5,000 years. Fertile areas of the region also produce olives, olive oil, nuts, spices and Arabica coffee.

Depending on water

Rivers supply many other needs as well as providing the water itself. Boats use waterways to transport goods. Engineers dam rivers to generate hydro-electric power. Water is often too scarce to meet public demand. One way to get more fresh water is to remove salt from sea water. However this process, called desalination, is expensive. Water use is a difficult political issue in the region. Turkey, Syria and Iraq all share the river basin of the Tigris and Euphrates. This has led to disputes between them about dams and irrigation schemes.

▼ Palestinians harvest watermelons near Jericho (Ariha). This area of the River Jordan's West Bank (see pages 40–41) is fertile and green, with a mild climate.

▲ Syrian villagers wash their clothes at a well. Water supplies are essential for human health and hygiene. The Middle East and North Africa have five per cent of the world's population, but less than one per cent of the world's water. In Syria, 94 per cent of scarce water resources are used for farming, four per cent for the home and two per cent for industrial use.

Growing crops

Farming first developed over 10,000 years ago in the river valleys of the Tigris, Euphrates and Nile, because of the fertile soil left behind by flooding (see pages 16–17). Much of the region is drier now, but crops still need water as well as soil. They depend on irrigation in drier areas and on springs or wells at desert oases. Today, Middle Eastern farmers cultivate wheat, barley, beans and rice. Olives and citrus fruits are grown in Mediterranean lands, while desert oases produce dates, melons and figs.

Industry – and oil

People in the Middle East make their living in many different ways. Cotton is a vital crop and the textile industry is important. An Omani may be a fisherman, while a Turk may work in a car factory. A Jordanian or Egyptian may run a tourist hotel. Gulf citizens may work in banks or airports.

Oil – the 'black gold' – is the most important industry. The Middle East has at least 66 per cent of the world's known oil reserves. Oil creates great wealth, but this is not shared out fairly among the people of the Middle East and poverty is widespread. Oil is so valuable to the rest of the world – as fuel and raw material for manufacturing – that it has created political problems in the region ever since it was discovered there, leading to invasions and wars.

▼ At a refinery, crude oil is processed and graded for use as fuels, lubricants, chemicals or plastics. This refinery is in Kuwait, where oil makes up 95 per cent of the country's export wealth. However, most of its workers are foreigners.

▶ Delicate jewellery has been produced by Middle Eastern goldsmiths for thousands of years and sold in bazaars. These bracelets and pendants are on sale at Dubai, in the United Arab Emirates, a popular tourist destination.

Hopes and fears

The Middle East is often in the news for many reasons. The price of oil and gas is always important to the rest of the world. There are deep-rooted political problems and ongoing crises. Recently there have been wars, rebellions, terrorist attacks and occupations by foreign troops. However, it is easy to forget that the region's peoples have always been great survivors of hardship. Young people here are talented and energetic and full of hope for the future. Theirs is a story that needs telling.

▲ Two young Iranian women show off inky forefingers. They have just placed their prints on ballot papers in the 2005 presidential election. The second round of voting saw a high turnout of 62 per cent. The presidency was won by Mahmoud Ahmadinejad, former mayor of Tehran.

◀ Demonstrators in Beirut, Lebanon, protest against the assassination of former Prime Minster Rafik Hariri in 2005. Many believed that Syrian agents were responsible for the murder.

Political problems

After the age of empires, the Middle East was in a weakened state. In the 20th century, powerful nations such as Britain, France, the Soviet Union (now Russia) and the USA all tried to control the resources of the region. To do this, they often supported governments that were undemocratic or unjust. The ancient homeland of the Kurds was divided up by new national borders. The foundation of Israel in 1948 also marked the start of decades of violence across the Middle East.

Rule and misrule

New Middle Eastern countries were created in the 20th century. Few have become democracies. Kings, presidents or religious leaders often held great personal power and suppressed all opposition. Some governments, including democratic ones, ruled with harshness or even terror. Some rebel organizations have used terror tactics, both within the Middle East and in many other parts of the world.

Peace with justice?

Western countries sometimes demand that Middle Eastern countries adopt western forms of government. Critics reply that the peoples of the Middle East should be free to devise their own forms of government and law. Many religious Muslims dislike western materialism and business methods. They want to see their countries run on strict Islamic principles. However, there are also divisions within Islam.

Some people argue that one way forward for the troubled Middle East is for international law and human rights to be respected. That should apply not just to terrorist organizations, but equally to Middle Eastern governments and to foreign governments who intervene in the region. The peoples of the Middle East deserve peace, justice and prosperity.

▲ A young girl does her classwork at a school for street children in Kabul, Afghanistan. She is a symbol of hope for the future in a country that has seen decades of civil war and the banning, by extreme Islamists, of education for females.

▼ American bombs set Baghdad ablaze at the start of the Iraq War in 2003. The United States and Britain claimed that the brutal Iraqi dictator Saddam Hussein was developing weapons of mass destruction, and invaded Iraq. No such weapons were ever found. The country has descended into a period of violence and chaos.

SUMMARY OF CHAPTER 1: PEOPLE AND PLACES

Land and people

The region known as the Middle East can be defined in various ways. The countries described in this book cover an area of about 9.6 million km^2 and are home to over 340 million people. These belong to many different ethnic groups, such as Arabs, Jews, Turks, Persians (Iranians) and Kurds, and speak many different languages. Faiths, which include Islam, Christianity, Judaism and Zoroastrianism, play an important part in everyday life and in the politics of the region.

These glass beads were traded by
the ancient Phoenicians 2,000 years ago.

A long history

The Middle East includes large deserts and many places experience extreme temperatures. However, it was here that farming first developed over 9,000 years ago, in the valleys of great rivers such as the Tigris, Euphrates and Nile. Villages, towns and then cities were built. Huge empires grew up, ruled by powerful kings. Great civilizations were developed by the Sumerians, Egyptians, Babylonians, Hittites, Assyrians and Persians. Many inventions that changed the world took place in the Middle East in ancient times. The Islamic states of the Middle Ages have also left a rich cultural legacy, with splendid mosques, fine textiles and metalwork, beautiful poetry and music. The 20th century saw powerful nations from outside the Middle East, such as Great Britain, France, Russia and the United States, attempting to control the region, which holds the world's biggest known oil reserves. It also saw the creation of new, independent nations, including Israel in 1948. The Middle East has experienced rapid modernization, religious and political unrest and terrible warfare in the last 50 years. Its peoples need peace and hope for the future.

Go further...

 Read about the history of the Ottoman empire at www.bbc.co.uk/ religion/religions/islam/ history/ottoman/index.shtml

Mosque by David Macaulay (Houghton Mifflin, 2003)

Life in Ancient Mesopotamia by Lynn Peppas and Shilpa Mehta-Jones (Crabtree Publishing Company, 2004)

The Kingfisher Book of Religions by Trevor Barnes (Kingfisher, 1999)

The Arabian Nights edited by Fiona Waters and illustrated by Christopher Corr (Chrysalis Children's Books, 2002)

Archaeologist
Studies ancient ruins and physical remains in a scientific way, to find out about the past.

Ecologist
Studies the relationship between living things and the environment.

Egyptologist
Studies all aspects of life and death in ancient Egypt.

Historian
Studies past events by looking at written or visual records.

Linguist
Studies ancient or modern languages and may work as an interpreter.

 See a fantastic collection of treasures from ancient Egypt and Mesopotamia at: The British Museum, Great Russell Street, London WC1B 3DG, UK. Telephone +44 (0) 20 7323 8299 www.thebritishmuseum.ac.uk

For excellent museums on Mesopotamia and on Islamic art, visit: The Pergamon Museum complex, Staatliche Museen zu Berlin, Genthiner Str. 38D-10785 Berlin, Germany. Telephone +49 (0) 30 266 2987 www.smb.spk-berlin.de

Explore the world's greatest collection of ancient Egyptian remains at: The Egyptian Museum, Cairo, Egypt, Midan El Thairir, Cairo, Egypt 11557 www.emuseum.gov.eg

CHAPTER 2

Modern nations

Sixteen independent Middle Eastern nations are featured in this chapter. They are Turkey, Syria, Lebanon, Israel, Egypt, Jordan, Saudi Arabia, Yemen, Oman, United Arab Emirates, Qatar, Bahrain, Kuwait, Iraq, Iran and Afghanistan. The Palestinian Territories, conquered by Israel in 1967, are not a nation in their own right but they have a degree of self-government and aim to achieve statehood soon. Some of the borders of the Middle Eastern nations follow natural features, such as rivers. Many more borders are the result of historical treaties or conquests. The Middle Eastern nations have many different kinds of government. Some are democracies, with a choice of political parties. Others are governed by all-powerful royal families or by dictators.

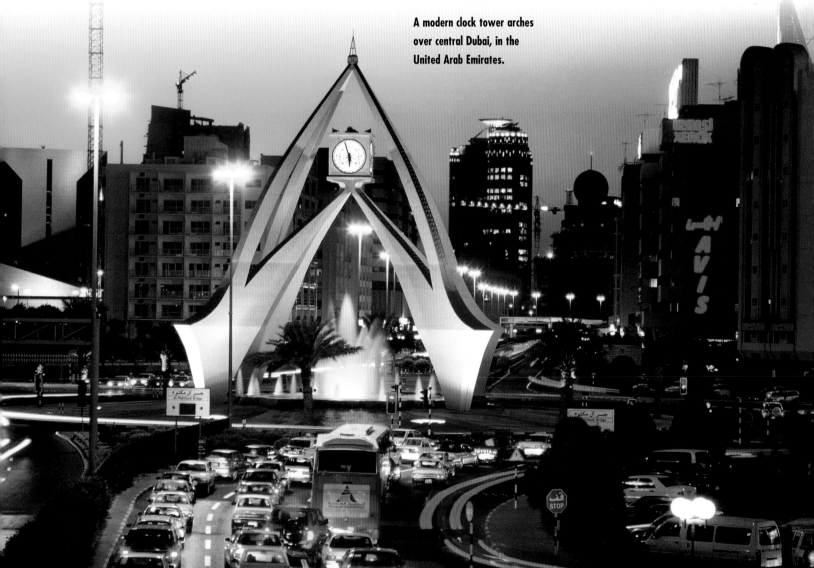

A modern clock tower arches over central Dubai, in the United Arab Emirates.

International co-operation

No countries exist in isolation. The nations of the Middle East have, over the ages, shared much of their history and culture. Many have similar advantages, such as oil resources, and disadvantages, such as a shortage of water. However, shared experiences have not always led to greater peace or understanding within the region, and wars have been all too common. The Iran-Iraq war of 1980 to 1988, a bitter dispute about the border between the two countries, may have killed close to 2 million people – with no lasting gains for either side.

Political and economic ties

There are many political, economic and military groupings in the Middle East. The Arab League includes all the Arab countries in the region and beyond. It concerns itself with defence, economics, communications, culture, labour, agriculture and the environment. International trading groups such as the Organization of Petrol Exporting Countries (OPEC) also influence the region's economics.

▼ Helping hands… An Iranian relief worker directs a Danish search and rescue team to a collapsed house after the terrible earthquake at Bam, Iran, in December 2003. Iran and its neighbours all lie in earthquake danger zones. Expert teams from many countries helped with the rescue effort after this disaster. The co-operation goes both ways, as aid workers from the Middle East have a role in disaster relief elsewhere in the world.

▲ United Nations troops have served as peace-keepers in many Middle Eastern trouble spots. These soldiers are shown working in Nicosia, Cyprus, in 1996. Their job was to guard the line that divided the Republic of Cyprus from the unrecognized Republic of Northern Cyprus, founded after a Turkish invasion in 1974.

The international arena

All the nations of the Middle East are members of the United Nations (UN). UN agencies work for health, human rights, refugee support, education, science, culture, children's rights and industrial development all over the world. The UN has also been involved in major political decisions, such as the founding of Israel in 1948 and economic sanctions against Iraq from 1990 to 2003. Voluntary organizations are also active in the Middle East, undertaking work in disaster relief or human rights.

Building bridges

Shared sporting or cultural interests can bring nations together. The Asian Football Confederation calls football 'Asia's unifying passion'. Music may also serve as a route to international understanding. Asian folk music and western pop music may blend and feed into each other. Cinema-goers in the USA or Europe may watch a film from Iran or Turkey.

▲ The flags of the Red Cross and the Red Crescent are symbols of international assistance in times of war, conflict and disaster. This non-political international federation provides medical assistance and also monitors conditions for prisoners of war. The cross is a Christian symbol and the crescent a Muslim one, so a new, non-religious symbol of a crystal shape is now sometimes used.

▲ The Iranian women's football team (in red) takes on the Palestinians (in white and blue) during a championship in Jordan in 2005. Sports often help to further international relations and are also helping to provide a less traditional role for women.

Turkey

Turkey is the westernmost nation in the Middle East. It lies on the border of Europe, and has coasts on the Black Sea and the Mediterranean. Summers are hot and dry, but winters can be snowy and bitterly cold. Much of its area is taken up by the broad peninsula of Anatolia, a plateau ringed by mountain ranges and lakes. The population numbers over 70 million and is made up chiefly of Turks, with a large Kurdish minority. Large cities include Istanbul and Ankara, the capital. People may be employed in car manufacture, tourism, or growing fruit, olives and cereal crops.

▶ Members of a Turkish family gather for an open-air meal. Grilled lamb, chicken or fish are popular choices. Meat may be cooked on skewers as kebabs. These women are wearing headscarves, which is common in the countryside, but Turkish women in government jobs and girls at school are not allowed to wear this traditional headgear.

▶ Robes swirl as the Mevlevi or 'whirling dervishes' spin around at Konya, in Anatolia, Turkey. This form of dancing is part of the mystical Sufi tradition of Islam and is a form of meditation. The Mevlevi revere as their founder the great poet and teacher Celaleddin Rumi (1207–73).

Turkey's past

In prehistoric times, Anatolia played a pioneering role in the development of agriculture, towns and metalworking. Çatal Hüyük was already a major town about 8,000 years ago. The region was later ruled by Hittites, Persians, Greeks and Romans, and was the centre of the Byzantine empire. In the Middle Ages, it was settled by waves of Turkish peoples, such as the Seljuks and Ottomans. Istanbul was capital of the Ottoman empire from 1453 until 1923, when Turkey became a republic.

▲ Turkish schoolchildren hold up paper masks in memory of Mustafa Kemal (1881–1938), known as 'Atatürk' (meaning 'Father of Turks'), who founded the Turkish republic. He created a modern state in which religion was separated from government. He is still greatly admired today.

Turkey and Cyprus

The Mediterranean island of Cyprus was once part of the Ottoman empire, then was ruled by the British from 1878 to 1960. Today it is an independent republic. Geographically part of Asia, Cyprus is home to ethnic Greeks and ethnic Turks. Following years of conflict between these groups, the north of the island was invaded by Turkish troops in 1974, dividing the country. A breakaway Turkish Republic of Northern Cyprus was formed, but is not officially recognized internationally.

Modern Turkey

Turkey modernized rapidly in the 20th century. Many of the country's Kurds have been unhappy with Turkish rule, and this has often led to violence. The government has sometimes been accused of human-rights abuses. Today, the Turkish government is applying to join the European Union (EU).

▶ A family harvests lemons at Lapithos in the north of Cyprus, an area invaded by Turkish forces in 1974. The economy of the island as a whole depends on its sunny climate, which produces grapes, citrus fruit, olives, wheat and tobacco, and attracts many tourists.

Syria

To the south of Turkey, Syria stretches all the way from the Mediterranean coast to the borders of Jordan and Iraq. Syria has a rich history of trade, craft and religion dating back thousands of years. Its capital, Damascus, can claim to be the oldest continuously inhabited city in the world. Syria's main geographical regions are the fertile coastal plain, which supports olive groves and other farming land, mountain ranges running parallel to the coast, and to the east and south, the arid wilderness of the Syrian desert, crossed by the Euphrates or al-Furat river.

▲ The massive stone castle of Krak des Chevaliers is a reminder of the stormy history of Syria in the Middle Ages. Its walls still tower over the valley between Homs and Tripoli. Krak served as a fortress of the Kurds in the 11th century CE. In the 13th century, it was rebuilt by Christian crusaders, knights from Europe who fought against Muslims for control of the region.

Syria's place in history

Syria was part of the great empires that governed the Middle East in ancient times. In about 1750BCE, the Babylonians ruled the land. They were followed by invading armies of Hittites, Assyrians, Persians, Greeks and Romans. Syria was an early centre of Christianity and this continued through the period of Byzantine rule, ending with the Arab conquest of 634CE. The country was ruled by Ottoman Turks from 1516 to 1918. Full independence did not come until 1946. Today Syria is a republic.

Modern Syria

Most Syrians live in the west of the country. Nine out of ten are Arabs, and Arabic is the most common language. There are also Armenian and Kurdish communities. Six million people live in the ancient city of Damascus. Many Syrians work in the oil industry, in clothing manufacture and in processing foods. Farmers grow cotton, olives and lentils, and raise sheep or goats.

◀ Cloth is block-printed by hand in the northern city of Aleppo (al-Halab in Arabic). Syria has long been famous for its textiles, producing wool, linen, cotton and silk. One patterned weave became known as 'damask', named after the city of Damascus.

Political tensions

Syrian politics have been controlled by the Ba'th Party since 1963. The Golan Heights region has been occupied by Israel since the Six-Day War of 1967. Syria's relations with Israel and Lebanon are a great source of tension. Syria has also protested against Turkish use of water from the Euphrates.

◀ Syrian troops withdraw from eastern Lebanon in 2005, after nearly 30 years of intervention in that country's affairs. Syria plays a key role in Middle Eastern politics and its support is essential for any general peace agreement in the region.

▼ Religious buildings have occupied this site in Damascus for at least 3,000 years. This is the Umayyad mosque, founded in 706CE when the city was at the height of its power in the Muslim world. It has been rebuilt several times.

Lebanon

Lebanon is a small country on the eastern shores of the Mediterranean Sea, a region once known as the Levant. A coastal strip rises to mountains that run parallel to the coast. Eastward lies the fertile Bekaa valley and the Litani river. Summers in Lebanon are hot, but the short winters are mild and rainy. Farmers grow wheat, citrus fruits, grapes and olives. Today, Lebanon is rebuilding after civil war in the 1970s and 1980s.

The land of cedars

In ancient times, Lebanon's coast was the home of Phoenician seafarers. From ports such as Tyre and Sidon, they traded in cedar wood from the country's forests, which were then very large, and in an expensive purple dye. Romans came to the region in the first century BCE, and Arabs in the 7th century CE. Lebanon became part of the Ottoman empire in 1516. It was governed by France from 1920 to 1941 and became independent in 1943. Lebanon fought its neighbour Israel in 1948, and in the years that followed many Palestinian refugees settled here.

◀ A sea of Lebanese flags marks a large demonstration in Beirut in 2005. Protestors hold up portraits of former prime minister Rafik Hariri, who was assassinated. The protestors blamed Syrian agents for his death and called, successfully, for Syrian troops to be withdrawn from Lebanon.

◀ Worshippers light candles at a Greek Orthodox church in Beirut. Lebanon is also home to Armenian and Syrian Orthodox churches and to Maronite, Melkite, Catholic and Coptic churches.

▶ Grapes ripen in the sun at a vineyard at Mansoura, in the Bekaa valley. Wine has been produced in Lebanon for over 5,000 years.

Peoples and faiths

The chief cities of Lebanon, Tripoli and Beirut, are on the coast. Lebanon is a country of many religions. It has been described as having an 'Arab face'; Islam is the most common religion and Arabic is the chief language. The Druze faith, a breakaway sect of Islam, has its followers too. There is a large Armenian community. There is also a large minority of Christians (about 40 per cent of the population), belonging to many different sects, such as the Maronites.

Chaos and order

From 1975 to 1990, civil war raged in Lebanon. Christians and Muslims fought each other and Israel invaded from the south. Beirut became known for its violence and chaos. Syrian troops intervened in 1976. The 1990s saw a return to greater order and reconstruction of the capital. The Israelis withdrew in 2000. Syrian troops finally withdrew in 2005, but mistrust of Syria remained widespread.

◀ Peace returns to Lebanon as walkers, rollerbladers and street vendors take a promenade along the Corniche, the palm-lined seafront in Beirut. With its sunny climate and coast, Lebanon has great potential as a tourist destination, if it remains stable and peaceful.

Israel

Israel, on the southeastern coast of the Mediterranean, extends from Lebanon in the north to a short stretch of the Red Sea coast in the south. Its landscape includes highlands, desert and limited areas of fertile farmland. Israel exports oranges and vegetables, and industrial products such as textiles and cut diamonds. Israel occupies much of the region sometimes known as Palestine or the Holy Land, an area important to Jews, Christians and Muslims. Many of the political tensions in the Middle East today are concerned with the national status of Israel, or the location of its borders.

▲ A traditional ram's horn or shofar is blown to mark Rosh Hashanah, the Jewish New Year. Meals served at this time include apples and honey, symbols of sweetness in the year to come. Jews believe that the land of Israel was promised to them by God in ancient times.

An ancient history

The Hebrews, the ancient Jewish people, founded kingdoms called Israel and Judah in Palestine in the 11th and 10th centuries BCE. Babylonians, Persians, Greeks and Romans later invaded the region. In 70CE, a Jewish revolt against Roman rule was crushed and many Jews were forced into exile. Their descendants came to live in other parts of Asia, in North Africa, Europe and the Americas. Amongst many later conquerors of Palestine were Muslim Arabs, who increasingly settled the region from the 7th century CE.

▲ In 1967, young Palestinians who have fled from fighting in the Six-Day War between Israel and its Arab neighbours Egypt, Jordan and Syria, gather in a refugee camp at al-Mafraq, in Jordan. The fate of the Palestinian people, and the borders and status of any future Palestinian state, remain uncertain today.

The state of Israel

In the late 19th century, Jewish nationalists in Europe, called Zionists, decided to recolonize their ancient homeland. In 1918, Ottoman rule ended and from 1920 the British governed Palestine on behalf of the international League of Nations. Jewish settlers arrived from all over the world, especially after the terrible persecution and murder of Jews in Europe in the 1930s and 40s. In 1948, the United Nations recognized Israel as an independent nation.

Years of crisis

Many Palestinian Arabs were forced to leave the country when Israel was set up. Arab states declared war on the new state. Then, in the Six-Day War of 1967, Israel captured East Jerusalem, the West Bank region, the Gaza Strip, the Sinai desert and Syria's Golan Heights (see page 41). Israel's occupation and settlement of the West Bank, East Jerusalem (and Gaza until 2005) was opposed by Palestinians. Some Palestinians have launched terrorist attacks in Israeli cities, and Israel has attacked Palestinians. Attempts to secure a peaceful future for the region have so far failed.

▲ Israeli conductor and pianist Daniel Barenboim is a campaigner for peace. Here he performs at Ramallah, in the West Bank, in 2005. His West-Eastern Divan Orchestra is made up of young people from both Israel and Arab countries. He aims to increase understanding, friendship and co-operation across the political, ethnic and religious divisions of the Middle East.

▲ An Orthodox Jew in Jerusalem wears the dress of the mystical Hasidic tradition, which originated in central Europe. He is pointing out to his sons the Western Wall, one of Judaism's holiest sites, and the Dome of the Rock, which is sacred to Muslims. Both Israelis and Palestinians claim Jerusalem (also known as Yerushalayim or al-Quds) as their capital.

▲ An Arab sells fruit and vegetables at a market in the Old City of Jerusalem. Produce of the region includes tomatoes, aubergines, peppers, green beans, melons, figs and olives. Foods popular with both Jews and Arabs include falafel (chickpea balls) and shashlik (grilled meat on a skewer). Both Jews and Muslims have strict rules about the preparation of food and neither will eat pork.

Palestinian Territories

The Palestinian National Authority was set up in 1994–95. It governs about 15 per cent of the land which made up Palestine before 1948. At the moment these territories are not recognized as an independent state, but most peace plans propose that the area should be the basis of a Palestinian state. It is currently made up of two territories. Gaza is a narrow strip of arid land bordering Egypt and the Mediterranean. The West Bank borders the Jordan river and the Dead Sea.

▲ Palestinians wait at an Israeli army checkpoint in 2002. This was at the height of the second uprising, or intifada (meaning 'shaking off'). At this time of tension, Israeli troops made many incursions into (sudden attacks on) the Palestinian Territories.

Jerusalem

The city of Jerusalem is sacred to three faiths: Judaism, Christianity and Islam. It is claimed as a capital by both Israelis and Palestinians. Does it have a shared future, or could it perhaps be designated as an international 'holy city'? The question of Jerusalem arouses very strong emotions. No solution that is acceptable to both sides has yet been proposed.

▼ In 2002 Israel began the construction of a long barrier of fences and high concrete walls. Israelis claimed this was to provide security against Palestinian terror attacks. However, sections of the wall passed through Palestinian territory. Palestinians claimed the real aim of the Israelis was to annexe, or take possession of, more land from the West Bank.

Jerusalem

Muslim Quarter

Christian Quarter

TEMPLE MOUNT

Church of the Holy Sepulchre

Western (Wailing) Wall

Dome of the Rock

al-Aqsa Mosque

Jewish Quarter

Armenian Quarter

▲ The Old City shown on this map is just one small part of the big modern city. It lies within East Jerusalem, and was ruled by Jordan before 1967. It is now governed by Israel, but citizens of East Jerusalem were allowed to vote in the Palestinian elections in 2006.

◄ Wadi al-Qelt is a fertile oasis on the West Bank. Since ancient times its natural springs have been used for irrigation or been carried along aqueducts (water channels) to the city of Jericho.

Troubled years

After the new Israeli state was set up in 1948, Gaza was administered by Egypt, while the West Bank and East Jerusalem became part of Jordan. Israel's defeat of these countries in the Six-Day War of 1967 led to Israeli occupation of these and other territories. Jewish settlers began to build towns in the conquered lands, which was against international law. Some groups within the Palestinian Liberation Organization, which had been founded in 1964, began campaigns of terrorism against Israel. There began a long cycle of violence, terror and retaliation by both Palestinians and Israeli troops. In 2005, Israel withdrew its settlers from Gaza.

From 2004 to 2006, a series of events made the future of the peace process uncertain. These included the death of Palestinian president Yasser Arafat, a stroke suffered by Israeli prime minister Ariel Sharon and the election win of the radical Islamist Hamas party in the Palestinian Territories.

The Palestinians

Palestinian Arabs make up the majority of the population of the Palestinian Territories, with Jewish settlers now accounting for 17 per cent of the West Bank population. The Palestinians are mostly Muslim, although about six per cent are Christian. Farmers produce olives for oil, dates and citrus fruits. Industries process foods and produce soap, cement and textiles.

Israel 1948 to present
- Israel 1948
- Israeli conquests 1967
- — Israel's border 2006
- --- Israel's border 2006 – disputed

► The Israeli-occupied West Bank and Gaza were given limited self-rule under a Palestinian National Authority in 1994–1995.

Beirut

Damascus

S Y R I A

LEBANON

Mediterranean

Golan Heights

◄ The Golan Heights are part of Syria but occupied by Israel.

Sea

Haifa

Sea of Galilee

West Bank

Tel Aviv

Jaffa

Jordan

Amman

Jerusalem

Jericho

Gaza

Gaza

Dead Sea

Hebron

Port Said

Rafah

ISRAEL

J O R D A N

Jordan

Sinai Peninsula

Eilat

▲ The Sinai Peninsula was occupied by Israel from 1967 to 1982, when it was returned to Egypt.

Suez Canal

Gulf of Suez

Gulf of Aqaba

SAUDI ARABIA

E G Y P T

Egyptian

Egypt is an African country, but it has had close links with southwest Asia for thousands of years and so it is also generally considered to be part of the Middle East. This is a land of shimmering hot, sandy deserts and palm-fringed oases. Flowing through it all is the River Nile, on its 6,695-km journey from central Africa to the Mediterranean coast, where it forms a lush delta region. To the east is the Red Sea, linked to the Mediterranean by the Suez Canal. Egypt's major cities include Cairo, the capital, and the ancient city of Alexandria.

▲ Crowds jostle in the streets of the Egyptian capital, Cairo (al-Qahira). This is the biggest urban centre in Africa. It has a population of about 8 million living in the city itself and perhaps a further 8 million in the greater Cairo area. Cairo is a city of hotels and embassies, hooting traffic, mosques, minarets and street markets. It has a huge bazaar called Khan al-Khalili.

◄ An Egyptian wall painting illustrates the link between Egypt and the rest of the Middle East. It features Arabic writing and depicts the hajj, the annual pilgrimage of faithful Muslims to Mecca in Saudi Arabia. Fasts, festivals and pilgrimage mark out the Islamic year.

► Wooden boats called feluccas sail downstream near the southern town of Aswan. Sailing boats may have been used on the River Nile for about 6,000 years. The river's flow is now controlled by the massive Aswan High Dam, completed in 1970.

Land of the pyramids

The civilization that thrived from around 3000BCE for over 2,000 years, with its awe-inspiring pyramids and temples, still impresses the world today. It was followed by Persian, Ptolemaic, Roman and Byzantine rule. The Arab conquest of 641CE introduced Islam to the land. Egypt became part of the Ottoman empire in 1517, France invaded in 1798 and in 1882 Britain occupied the country. In 1956, Britain withdrew troops from Egypt as the country began to emerge as a strong regional power under Gamal Abd al-Nasser.

Modern Egypt

Various attempts to unite Egypt with Libya and Syria failed. Much of Egypt's history since 1948 has been dominated by military conflict with its neighbour, Israel, but a peace treaty was signed in 1979. This triggered unrest amongst many groups, including Islamists, who assassinated President Anwar Sadat in 1981. His successor Hosni Mubarak has been criticized for suppressing opposition. Egypt is one of the key countries in the politics of the Arab world and of the Middle East as a whole.

◀ An oil pipeline snakes throughout the desert near the Iraqi border, in the northeast of Saudi Arabia. Ninety per cent of Saudi Arabia's export earnings come from oil and natural gas. Most Saudi oil is shipped out in supertankers through the Persian Gulf.

▲ Traditional pastimes such as falconry (hunting with birds of prey) are still very popular across the Arabian peninsula. Although wealthy Saudis own expensive cars and luxurious palaces, many still admire the way of life of the desert nomads. Traditions such as loyalty and lavish hospitality are very important to them.

Saudi life

Oil riches have transformed Saudi Arabia. There are now gleaming modern cities and airports, although many ordinary people remain poor. Many foreigners work in Saudi Arabia, including large numbers from South Asia.

Saudi Arabia has remained a conservative country. Traditional dress, ideal for hot, dusty deserts, is common. Men wear an ankle-length tunic (thobe) and a head-scarf (ghutra) secured by cord. Women wear a thobe over trousers and a black cloak (abaya), and cover their faces with a veil or mask. Western dress can also be seen in the cities.

Political issues

The Saudi royal family is large, incredibly rich and holds great power. No political parties are allowed in Saudi Arabia. Punishments are severe even for minor offences. Alcohol is strictly banned. The government has come under criticism from some Muslims for allowing non-Muslim troops on Saudi soil. It has also been criticized internationally for its failure to support human rights and democracy.

Yemen and Oman

The southern coast of the Arabian peninsula consists of two small states, Yemen and Oman. Yemen borders the Red Sea and the Gulf of Aden. Only a narrow strait, the Bab al-Mandab, separates it from Africa. Yemen is a land of desert and dusty plains, rising to mountains in the south and west. The southwest has the highest rainfall, and most of the country's people live there. Oman is another land of deserts, with mountain ranges in the north. Its coastline runs along the Gulf of Oman. A further patch of Omani territory occupies the Musandam peninsula, at the entrance to the Persian Gulf.

▲ Yemeni territory includes the beautiful tropical island of Socotra, 350km to the south of the mainland, in the Indian Ocean. The island has many unique plant and animal species. This blossom belongs to a form of desert rose that is found only on this island. Its thick, bottle-shaped trunk acts a store for water.

▼ A herder waters his cattle at a communal pool in the town of Hababa, to the northwest of Sana, Yemen's capital. The classic Yemeni houses, multi-storeyed and flat-roofed, with decorative windows, are much better suited to the climate and geology of the region than modern concrete buildings.

The land of Sheba

Yemen's position at the entrance to the Red Sea made it an early centre of Asian and African trade. Yemen was part of several ancient kingdoms, such as Saba or Sheba in the 10th century BCE. Islam arrived in 628CE and continued to thrive over the centuries under the rule of Egyptians, Ottoman Turks and tribal leaders. In 1839, Britain took over the city of Aden, and this became an important port of call for ships when the Suez Canal opened 30 years later. The 20th century was marked by warfare against the British, and by a bitter civil war between royalists and republicans. Out of the chaos, there emerged two rival, independent states in the north and south, which finally united in 1990.

Qat and coffee

Most Yemenis are farmers or herders. The green southwest of the country produces wheat and millet, fruit and tomatoes. Cotton is grown and so is qat, a shrub whose leaves, chewed, are used as a mild drug. Coffee was probably discovered in Ethiopia, but early in its long history the coffee from the Arabian peninsula became the finest known. 'Mocha' coffee takes its name from the port of al-Mukha. Yemen also produces and refines oil.

▲ Smiling Omani children peek out of a latticed window. Oman has fewer resources than some of its neighbours, but oil wealth has helped to build more schools in the towns and greatly increase the number who can read and write. Children's healthcare has also greatly improved since the 1970s.

▲ Green fields are a rare sight in Oman. These terraced slopes were built by farmers on the edge of a canyon at Sayq, to the northeast of Nazwa. Here, in the northern mountain range of Jabal al-Akhdar, the climate is cooler and water is carefully conserved.

Muscat and Oman

Merchants may have been sailing along the Omani coast for 5,000 years. Arabs settled the region in the 9th century BCE and for many centuries Persia (Iran) ruled the north of Oman. Islam became the principal faith from 630CE. Muscat, Oman's capital, and part of the coast were held by the Portuguese from 1507 to 1650. The Omani sultans (rulers) were at the height of their power in the early 19th century. Muscat and Oman came under British control in the later 19th century, and independence was not won back until 1951. Oil was discovered in 1964, and the wealth it created transformed this desert land into a modern state.

The Sultanate today

Omanis are still a seafaring people, and many coastal villagers live by fishing. On land, the produce includes limes, melons and dates, but farming depends on very limited irrigation. Oil and gas are the major industries. The Sultans of Oman have great power and there are no official political parties in the country. Traditions are highly valued. The national emblem is the khanjar, an ornate curved dagger worn with traditional male dress.

The Gulf states

Four very small states are grouped around the western and southern shores of the Persian Gulf, along the Saudi Arabian border. They are Kuwait, Bahrain, Qatar and the United Arab Emirates (UAE). All are desert countries where oil and natural gas have funded the development of modern cities, businesses and airports. The Persian Gulf has been an important trading route since ancient times. The Gulf states have Muslim Arab populations, but also many foreign residents. All are kingdoms or emirates (countries ruled by princes called emirs) in which political parties play no part in government.

Kuwait

Beneath Kuwait's barren, featureless land lie enormous oil reserves. Kuwait has an estimated 10 per cent of the world's known reserves of crude oil. It is still recovering from the effects of the 1990 invasion by its neighbour Iraq. This invasion, led by the Iraqi dictator Saddam Hussein, and the war that followed, proved to be an economic and ecological disaster for Kuwait. In 2003, the country became a base for large numbers of US-led international forces that invaded Iraq.

▲ The luxury Burj al-Arab hotel towers over Jumeirah Beach, in Dubai, UAE. It is shaped like the sail of a dhow, the traditional trading ship of the Arab seafarers. Dubai's rapid development as a big city is remarkable, but the building of tourist attractions places a strain on fragile coastal and desert environments.

▼ Bahrain is a wealthy state and its ruling classes enjoy sports such as motor racing. Here Shaykh Fawaz bin Muhammad Al Khalifa greets Formula One World Champion Michael Schumacher before the desert Formula One Grand Prix outside Manama in 2004.

Bahrain

Bahrain is a sweltering island of rock surrounded by the turquoise waters of the Persian Gulf, linked by road to the mainland. Over the ages, it was ruled by Persians, Arabs, Portuguese and British. In 1968, it became part of a regional federation, but finally became a state in its own right in 1971. The oil reserves that created Bahrain's wealth are running low, and so new businesses and industries are now being developed.

▲ Workers at one of Kuwait's many modern oil rigs sink new pipes. Kuwait owns 10 per cent of the world's oil reserves and these are expected to last for about 100 years. Kuwait's oil industry employs thousands of foreign workers, mainly from southern Asia and other Arab nations.

▲ Al-Jazeera television journalists work from the station's newsroom in Doha, Qatar. This satellite news network began broadcasting in Arabic in 1996 and launched an English-language service in 2005. It is the only Arab-language news channel that is not state-owned, and has been hugely successful, despite attracting criticism from the United States and some Arab governments and Muslim organizations.

Qatar

Qatar is a peninsula lying between Bahrain and the UAE. It did not join a federation with its neighbours, and gained full independence from Britain on its own in 1971. It is a flat, dry, desert land with high reserves of oil and five per cent of the world's reserves of natural gas. Most of its wealth comes from these, and people in Qatar enjoy a high standard of living. Desalination converts sea water to fresh water. There are fisheries, but little farming is possible in this arid land.

United Arab Emirates

These desert emirates used to be known as the Trucial States, because they signed a peace treaty or 'truce' with Britain in the 19th century. They tried to form a federation with neighbouring states in 1968, but Bahrain and Qatar withdrew in 1971. The seven remaining emirates formed an independent country, made up of Abu Dhabi, Dubai, Sharjah, Ajman, Umm al-Qaiwan, Ras al-Khaimah and Fujairah. The land is parched but produces desert fruits such as dates, and the coast provides fishing. The UAE's great wealth derives from massive reserves of oil and gas. This has been used to develop business, commerce and tourism.

Iraq

Iraq consists of the lands around the rivers Tigris and Euphrates, which were known in ancient times as Mesopotamia. The rivers and the agricultural plains between them dominate central and southeastern Iraq. Northeastern Iraq is mountainous, while hot sandy deserts cover much of the sparsely populated western and southern regions. The capital, Baghdad, lies at the centre of the country and has a population of nearly 6 million. Iraq is a land of date palms, oil wells and oil pipelines, but its prosperity has been destroyed in recent years by dictatorship, sanctions, wars and violence.

◀ Kurdish farmers gather hay near the city of Arbil, in the mountainous northwest of Iraq. Iraq's Kurdish community has long campaigned for independence. It was persecuted under Saddam Hussein and so benefited greatly from his downfall in 2003. The Kurds now have a degree of autonomy or self-government.

The Iraqi people

More than three-quarters of Iraqis are Arabs, and Arabic is the official language, but there is a large minority of Kurds living in the north. Ninety-seven per cent of all Iraqis are Muslim, and there are both Shi'a and Sunni groups in Iraq (see pages 14–15). Kurdish Iraqis mostly belong to the Sunni Muslim minority, while most Arab Iraqis follow the Shi'a tradition of Islam. Unity of the new Iraq depends on the healing of old wounds between different groups.

The cradle of civilization

From about 3400BCE, Mesopotamia saw many advances in civilization, with the growth of great cities and empires (see pages 16–17). Sumerians, Assyrians and Babylonians ruled these lands, and they were followed by Persians, Greeks and Romans. Arab armies brought Islam in 637CE and founded an Islamic state or caliphate. In 750CE, with the rise of the Abbasid empire, Baghdad became a centre of Islamic culture and learning, and Iraq began a golden age of trade and prosperity. However, in later centuries it was weakened by Mongol invasions and in 1534 it became a backwater of the Ottoman Empire, ruled from Constantinople.

▶ Sunni and Shi'a Muslims join together in prayers at the Imam Musa Kazim mosque in Baghdad. If Iraq is to remain a single, united country, then ethnic and religious differences must be put aside and the increasing violence between the various different communities halted.

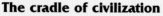

Kings and dictators

After World War I brought an end to the Ottoman empire, Iraq was under British control for a short time, then achieved independence, as a monarchy, in 1932. The king was overthrown in 1958 and, in 1963, a military coup brought the Ba'th party to power. From 1979, this party was led by Saddam Hussein, a dictator who crushed all political opposition and persecuted both Kurds and Shi'a Muslims. In 1980, a long and disastrous war began between Iraq and its neighbour Iran. Soon after this war came the Iraqi invasion of Kuwait in 1990. Iraqi troops were pushed back from Kuwait by an international, US-led coalition in 1991.

Iraq 2003–2005

⇨ Coalition ground attack

✸ Major flashpoints

▲ This map shows the invasion route taken by the US-led Coalition in 2003 and centres of conflict during the occupation that followed. For example, Fallujah saw half its homes destroyed and many people killed during a US operation in November 2004.

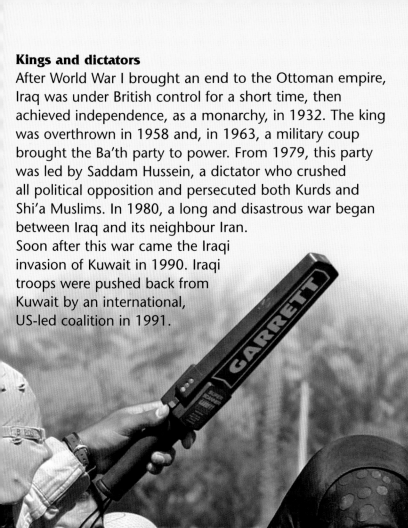

The Gulf wars

After 1991, there followed a long period of international sanctions against Iraq, restricting the trade of goods in and out of the country. This brought disease, poverty and even death to many Iraqi people. In 2003, US and British troops invaded Iraq, accusing Saddam Hussein of illegally developing weapons of mass destruction. The dictator was overthrown, but no weapons were ever found. There was growing violence and daily life remained wretched. Elections were held in 2005, but in 2006 Iraq was on the brink of civil war.

◄ A US soldier uses a metal detector to check women in Baghdad for weapons. By 2006 it was still unclear when foreign troops would withdraw from Iraq. Some politicians believed that they should stay until the country was stable, but others believed the presence of troops was the problem, not the solution.

Iran

I ran is the second largest nation in the Middle East, after Saudi Arabia. Before 1935, it was known as Persia and its history goes back thousands of years. Modern Iran stretches from Turkey to Pakistan, from the Caspian Sea to the Gulf coast. Its snowy mountains include the Elburz range to the north of the capital, Tehran, and the Zagros mountains. Iran's landscapes vary from rolling grasslands to expanses of desert, salt flats and seashores. Ethnic Iranians (or Persians) make up the largest part of the population.

◀ Young women walk pass the Sheikh Lotfollah mosque in Esfahan. This wonderful building was completed in 1619, in the reign of Shah Abbas I. It is covered in beautiful coloured tiles and intricate patterns made up of flowers and peacock tails.

▲ Mullahs (Muslim clerics) sit in the Esfahan sunshine. Most Iranians follow the Shi'a tradition of Islam, which differs from the mainstream Sunni tradition in its belief about the role of religious leaders (see page 15). The 1979 revolution handed over the government of Iran to religious leaders.

Ancient and medieval Persia

From 550 to 330 BCE, the vast Persian empire was the wonder of the ancient world, with its great armies and royal palaces. It was overthrown by the Greeks, but splendid new Persian empires arose in the 3rd to 7th centuries CE and again in the 16th to 18th centuries. Persia produced great poets, musicians, artists and craft workers. In the 19th century, European powers began to seek control of the region, which lay between the rival empires of British India, Russia and Turkey.

Shahs and mullahs

In 1925, an army colonel, Reza Khan, seized power and had himself crowned Shah (king) with British consent. He was replaced by his son, Reza Shah Pahlavi, in 1941. In 1979, the monarchy was ended by Islamists, who created a fiercely religious state. Eight years of terrible war with Iraq had a staggering cost of close to 2 million lives. Political reforms took place in Iran in the late 1990s, but there remains great tension between Iran and the United States.

▲ A fashionable young woman from Tehran puts on make-up while a friend looks on. Strict religious rules about clothes and cosmetics were introduced by religious authorities in the 1980s, but are increasingly challenged by young people in the cities.

Iranian life

Iran is rich in oil and gas reserves, and much of the country's economy is controlled by the government. Farming varies greatly from region to region, producing cereal crops such as wheat and barley in some parts, and rice and sugar cane in others. Sheep and goats are raised by herders, and common ingredients of Iranian cooking include lamb, rice, fruit and nuts. Some men wear robes and turbans, while others wear western dress. Women are expected to remain veiled in public.

▶ Most Iranian houses are built of concrete or mud brick, but at the village of Kandovan, to the southeast of Tabriz, people have carved dwellings from cones of volcanic rock. These have been occupied for eight centuries.

Afghanistan

Afghanistan lies at the crossroads of Asia, east of Iran, on the edge of the Middle East. Afghanistan's geographical position has resulted in a long history of military conflict, as powerful countries have tried to gain control of the region. The land is beautiful but bleak, with barren deserts, massive mountain ranges and white-water rivers rushing through ravines and gorges. These harsh landscapes have hindered farming, trade and communications, and the country remains very poor.

▲ Water is taken from a well outside the Friday mosque or Masjid-i-Jami', in the western city of Herat. Afghanistan remains in desperate need of reconstruction, development, healthcare and education.

Empires and warriors

In the sixth century BCE, Afghanistan was part of the first Persian empire. The region later came under the rule of Greeks, Indians and Persians. In the 19th century, the British and Russians competed to gain control over these lands, which lay between their two empires. In 1979, the Soviet Union (now Russia) invaded to support Afghanistan's communist government. It came under attack from Islamist guerrillas, many of them from countries including Pakistan and Saudi Arabia, and funded by the USA and western powers.

◄ Women and girls queue at a health clinic. Many women in Afghanistan wear the burkha, a tent-like robe and veil with a face panel made of mesh. Women suffered greatly during the period of rule by the Taliban, but women's rights have improved since 2001.

The ancient city of Herat saw fighting from 1979, during the Soviet occupation. The city was captured by the Taliban in 1995 and by the Northern Alliance in 2001.

The southern city of Kandahar was a Soviet centre of command in the 1980s and in the 1990s was the birthplace of the Taliban movement. The Kandahar region remains a flashpoint of troubles and fighting.

The mountainous border between Pakistan and Afghanistan is a centre of resistance to the government in Kabul.

Kabul is the capital of Afghanistan. It was occupied by Soviet troops from 1979 to 1989 and bitterly fought over by Islamist groups from 1992 to 1996. It was captured by the Northern Alliance in 2001 and is the centre of the government headed by Hamid Kharzai.

UZBEKISTAN
TAJIKISTAN
TURKMENISTAN
Mazar-e-Sharif
Kashmir
Herat
Tora Bora Mts
Khyber Pass
Kabul
Islamabad
A F G H A N I S T A N
Peshawar
IRAN
Kandahar
P A K I S T A N
Quetta

Modern times

In 1989, the Russians withdrew, amidst civil war. From 1996 one Islamist group known as the Taliban ('seekers of knowledge') controlled much of the country. They supported a strict interpretation of Islamic law. They carried out public executions, banned women's education and even music. Because Afghanistan was a base for the international terrorist group al-Qaeda, who carried out the terrorist attacks on New York and Washington in September 2001, the country was attacked and invaded by US troops and their allies in 2001. The Taliban were overthrown with the help of the Northern Alliance, an anti-Taliban federation. A democratic system of government was introduced, but regional warlords remain powerful.

Afghan life

Afghanistan is home to many different ethnic groups, including Pashtun, Tajiks, Turkmen, Hazara and Baluchis and speakers of Dari, the eastern form of Farsi (Persian). About 80 per cent of Afghanis are Sunni Muslims, whilst about 19 per cent are Shi'a. Barley, maize and rice are grown in valleys, and sheep, goats and camels are raised in most regions. The country's nearness to Central Asia, Iran and China gives it an important position in the routing of fuel pipelines.

▲ A tank of the Northern Alliance enters Kabul in 2001. The capture of the Afghan capital marked the end of Taliban rule. However, supporters of the Taliban were still fighting foreign troops in parts of the country in 2006.

SUMMARY OF CHAPTER 2: MODERN NATIONS

Resources and economics

The 16 Middle Eastern nations and the territories covered in this book share many problems, but also many advantages. Farming is often difficult in regions of water shortage, and irrigation is generally necessary. Common crops include citrus fruits, olives, cotton, melons and dates. The riches of the region come chiefly from huge reserves of oil and natural gas. However, in many of the lands there is considerable poverty alongside the pockets of wealth. Trading has always been at the centre of Middle Eastern life, and today this may take place in traditional souks and bazaars, or in the air-conditioned banks and airport lounges of the Gulf States.

A camel race gets off to a flying start in Saudi Arabia.

Political issues

Traditional and modern styles exist side by side in many aspects of Middle Eastern life, from clothing to architecture and transport. There is also often a deeper clash, between 'western' and traditional Islamic values. These may be questions of everyday customs, such as diet, the use of alcohol, methods of banking, the way in which people dress, or the role of women. There may be questions of government and law. Should states be founded on religious principles, as in Iran, or should state and religion be separated, as in Turkey? Religion itself is often a cause of division and violence. International disputes are centred upon Israel and the Palestinian Territories, Syria and Lebanon, Iraq, Iran and Afghanistan. Human rights are threatened in many parts of the region, from Egypt to Saudi Arabia. As elsewhere in the world, areas of concern include the treatment of prisoners, torture, capital punishment, freedom to vote, women's rights, censorship and corruption in public life. These types of problems cannot be solved quickly. The future of the region depends on peace, justice and genuine international understanding of the region with its marvellous history and potential for the future.

Go further...

 Find out about the latest news from the Middle East, and read children's own reports from the region at the BBC's children's news site: http://news.bbc.co.uk/cbbcnews/hi/world/default.stm

Mud City by Deborah Ellis (Oxford University Press, 2004)

Thura's Diary: My Life in Wartime Iraq by Thura al-Windawi, translated by Robin Bray (Puffin Books, 2004)

Eyewitness Islam by Philip Wilkinson (Dorling Kindersley, 2005)

Israel and Palestine by John King (Raintree, 2005)

 Economist Studies work, money, resources and production.

Interpreter Translates 'live' from one language to another, so that people who speak different languages can communicate face to face. Languages of the Middle East include Arabic, Hebrew, Turkish, Kurdish and Farsi (Persian).

Journalist Reports on news or covers other stories for newspapers or broadcasters.

Production engineer Is responsible for extracting oil or natural gas from land or the seabed.

Visit the Topkapi Palace Museum in Istanbul, formerly the home of Ottoman sultans: Topkapi Sarayi, Sultanahmet, Eminonu. Istanbul, Turkey. Telephone: +90 212 512 04 80 http://www.ee.bilkent.edu.tr/~history/topkapi.html

Find out more about Jordan's history at: Jordan Archaeological Museum, Citadel Hill, Amman, Jordan. Telephone + 962 4638795

For more information on places to see if you visit the Middle East, go to: http://www.middleeastuk.com/destinations/index.htm

Reference

Facts and figures

Which is the biggest country in the Middle East and which is the smallest? How are these nations governed? What are their ethnic and religious differences? What are their resources and what goods do they produce? Statistics help us to understand the background to many issues.

AFGHANISTAN
Area: 645,807km²
Population: 20,291,000 (2002 official estimate)
Capital: Kabul
Main languages: Pashto, Dari (Persian), Uzbek
Main religions: Sunni Islam, Shi'a Islam
Type of government: republic; government control not effective over the whole country
Main exports: opium (illegally exported), dried fruit and nuts, carpets and rugs, wool and hides, cotton, precious and semi-precious stones

BAHRAIN
Area: 694km²
Population: 651,000 (2001 census)
Capital: Manama
Main languages: Arabic, Urdu, Malayalam
Main religions: Shi'a Islam, Sunni Islam
Type of government: kingdom; constitutional monarchy
Main exports: petroleum, aluminium, textiles, basic manufactures

EGYPT
Area: 997,739km²
Population: 68,649,000 (2004 official estimate)
Capital: Cairo
Main language: Arabic
Main religions: Sunni Islam, Coptic Christianity
Type of government: republic; dictatorship
Main exports: petroleum and petroleum products, cotton yarn and textiles and clothing, basic manufactures, metal products, chemicals

IRAN
Area: 1,638,057km²
Population: 68,467,000 (2005 official estimate)
Capital: Tehran
Main languages: Farsi (Persian), Azeri, Kurdish
Main religions: Shi'a Islam, Sunni Islam, Bahai
Type of government: Islamic republic
Main exports: petroleum and natural gas, chemicals, carpets, fruits, pistachios, iron and steel

IRAQ
Area: 435,052km²
Population: 25,898,000 (2003 official estimate)
Capital: Baghdad
Main languages: Arabic, Kurdish
Main religions: Shi'a Islam, Sunni Islam
Type of government: republic; government control not effective over the country
Main exports: petroleum and petroleum products

ISRAEL
Area: 20,517km² (this area includes East Jerusalem and the Golan Heights)
Population: 6,864,000 (including East Jerusalem and the Golan Heights, 2004 official estimate)
Capital: Jerusalem
(Jerusalem is not recognized by the international community as Israel's capital. Almost all countries treat another city, Tel Aviv, as Israel's capital)
Main languages: Hebrew, Arabic
Main religions: Judaism, Sunni Islam, Christianity
Type of government: republic; democracy
Main exports: machinery and transport equipment, software, cut diamonds, chemicals, clothing, food (particularly fruit) and drinks

JORDAN
Area: 89,342km²
Population: 5,101,000 (2004 census)
Capital: Amman
Main language: Arabic
Main religion: Sunni Islam
Type of government: kingdom; partial democracy
Main exports: clothing, phosphates, fertilizer, potash, fruit, vegetables and nuts, manufactures, pharmaceuticals

KUWAIT
Area: 17,818km²
Population: 2,213,000 (2005 census provisional figure)
Capital: Kuwait City
Main language: Arabic
Main religions: Sunni Islam, Shi'a Islam
Type of government: emirate; partial democracy
Main exports: petroleum and petroleum products, fertilizers

LEBANON
Area: 10,452km²
Population: 3,754,000 (2004 government estimate)
Capital: Beirut
Main language: Arabic
Main religions: Shi'a Islam, Sunni Islam, Druze, Greek Orthodox, Maronite Christianity
Type of government: republic; democracy
Main exports: precious stones and jewellery, chemicals, consumer goods re-exports, foodstuffs, tobacco, construction materials, textiles, paper products

OMAN
Area: 309,500km²
Population: 2,341,000 (2003 census)
Capital: Muscat
Main languages: Arabic, Baluchi
Main religions: Ibadiyah Islam, Sunni Islam, Shi'a Islam
Type of government: sultanate; absolute monarchy
Main exports: petroleum, re-exports, fish, metals, textiles

QATAR
Area: 11,427km²
Population: 831,000 (2006 official estimate)
Capital: Doha
Main languages: Arabic, Urdu, Malayam
Main religion: Sunni Islam
Type of government: emirate; dictatorship
Main exports: petroleum, fertilizers, steel, chemicals

SAUDI ARABIA
Area: 2,240,000km²
Population: 22,674,000 (2004 census, provisional figure)
Capital: Riyadh
Main language: Arabic
Main religion: Sunni Islam
Type of government: kingdom; absolute monarchy
Main exports: petroleum, petrochemicals

SYRIA
Area: 185,180km² (this area includes areas of the Golan Heights occupied by Israel)
Population: 17,130,000 (2002 government source)
Capital: Damascus
Main languages: Arabic, Kurdish
Main religions: Sunni Islam, Shi'a Islam, Christianity
Type of government: republic; dictatorship
Main exports: crude petroleum and petroleum products, fruit and vegetables, textiles and fabrics (including cotton fibre), meat

TURKEY
Area: 774,815km²
Population: 71,789,000 (2004 official estimate)
Capital: Ankara
Main languages: Turkish, Kurdish
Main religion: Sunni Islam
Type of government: republic; democracy
Main exports: textiles and clothing, foodstuffs, iron and steel, transportation equipment

UNITED ARAB EMIRATES
Area: 83,600km²
Population: 4,041,000 (2003 government estimate)
Capital: Abu Dhabi
Main languages: Arabic, Hindi, Urdu, English
Main religions: Sunni Islam, Shi'a Islam, Hinduism
Type of government: federation of sovereign emirates
Main exports: crude and refined petroleum, natural gas, re-exports, dried fish, dates

YEMEN
Area: 527,970km²
Population: 19,722,000 (2004 census)
Capital: Sana
Main language: Arabic
Main religion: Sunni Islam
Type of government: republic; partial democracy
Main exports: petroleum, coffee, dried fish

WEST BANK AND GAZA (PALESTINIAN TERRITORIES)
Area: 6,020km²
Population: 3,762,000 (2004 census provisional figure)
Capital: the Palestinian Authority claims East Jerusalem as its capital; the centre of administration is Ramallah
Main language: Arabic
Main religions: Sunni Islam, various Christian churches
Type of government: republic, democracy
Main exports: olives, fruit, vegetables, flowers, limestone.

Glossary

administer
To govern, manage or organize.

alms
Money given to the poor, charity.

assassination
A murder for political reasons.

bazaar
A Middle Eastern market, open-air or covered.

calligraphy
Fine handwriting as a form of art.

caravan
A group of merchants and their pack-animals who travel together for safety.

caravanserai
A wayside building where members of a caravan can rest, feed, store their wares and stable their animals.

Christianity
A faith based upon the teachings of Jesus Christ, who was born in Bethlehem in about 6BCE. Christians believe that Jesus was the Son of God.

civil war
A war fought between groups of people in the same country.

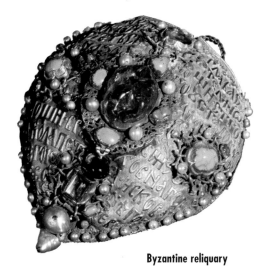

Byzantine reliquary

civilization
An advanced society with laws, government, arts and technologies.

cuneiform
'Wedge-shaped', a style of writing on clay tablets first developed in ancient Mesopotamia.

democracy
A system of government by elected representatives of the people.

desalination
Removing salt from sea water, so that it can be used for drinking.

dialect
A form of language other than the standard version, spoken regionally or by a particular group of people.

domesticate
To tame a wild animal such as a sheep or goat, so that it is of use to people.

Druze
The Druze are a group which broke away from mainstream Islam over 1,000 years ago. Most live in Lebanon, Syria and Israel.

economics
Matters of money, resources and work.

emirate
A state ruled by an emir, a traditional leader in the Arab world.

empire
A number of diffferent countries or peoples brought together under a single ruler.

ethnic group
A group of people, sometimes of shared descent, who share characteristics, such as social customs, language or religion.

federation
A group of different organizations that

Persian carpet

have joined together in a league. For example, the United Arab Emirates is a federation of countries.

fertile
Productive or rich (of soil), good for growing crops.

filigree
Delicate ornamental metalwork.

guerrilla
An irregular fighter who wears down the enemy with raids and surprise attacks rather than pitched battles.

hydro-electric power
Electrical power generated by water-driven turbines.

irrigation
Bringing water to crops by means of pipes or channels.

Islam
A faith based upon submision to the will of God (Allah). It was founded by the prophet Muhammad, who was born in Mecca in about 570CE.

Judaism
The faith of the Jewish people. It is based on laws believed to have been revealed by God to Moses in about the 14th century BCE.

millennium
A period of 1,000 years.

monsoon
A seasonal wind which blows across the Indian Ocean, bringing rain to the dry lands of southern Asia.

mosque
A place of worship for Muslims.

mullah
An Iranian cleric, an expert in the sacred laws of Islam. The word means 'teacher' or 'scholar'.

Muslim
A follower of Islam.

nomad
Someone who does not lead a settled existence, but travels with their herds from one pasture to another.

oasis
A spot in the desert where there is enough water for drinking, growing crops or watering animals.

pilgrim
Someone who undertakes a journey for religious reasons, travelling to a sacred place or shrine.

raw material
A basic substance which can be processed in order to manufacture goods.

refugee
Someone who is forced to flee from their home because of war, hunger or poverty.

republic
A country which has no king or queen but is ruled by representatives of the people.

resource
A natural substance which is of use to a country, such as water, timber, oil or coal.

sanctions
Restrictions placed on one country by others, in order to limit ability to trade, move freely or engage in other activities.

Shi'a
A branch of Islam which believes that Muhammad's cousin Ali was his true successor and that Shi'a leaders, called imams, are the messengers of God.

shofar
A ram's horn trumpet traditionally used in Jewish religious festivals.

souk
A Middle Eastern market, a bazaar.

Sufism
A mystic tradition in Islam associated with meditation, dance, chanting and poetry.

sultan
The king or ruler of an Islamic country.

Sunni
The mainstream branch of Islam. Sunnis honour four caliphs as the true successors of Muhammad and believe religious laws are to be made within the Islamic community.

synagogue
A Jewish place of worship.

terrorism
Using acts of extreme violence to create a climate of fear, and so bring about political change. Terrorism may be a policy of governments, of illegal armed groups and organizations, or of individuals.

United Nations (UN)
The world's largest international treaty organization, of which most nations are members. The UN, founded in 1945, promotes peace and cooperation. UN agencies act in areas including health, economic development and human rights.

ziggurat
A type of massive monument first built by the Sumerians, later by the Assyrians and Babylonians. Ziggurats were pyramids with terraced sides.

Zionist
A supporter of Jewish nationalism.

Zoroastrianism
A faith based on the teachings of Zoroaster, who lived in ancient Persia. Zoroastrians believe in one God and their sacred symbol is fire.

Assyrian carving showing chariot

Index

Acknowledgements

The publisher would like to thank the following for permission to reproduce their material. Every care has been taken to trace copyright holders. However, if there have been unintentional omissions or failure to trace copyright holders, we apologize and will, if informed, endeavour to make corrections in any future edition.

Key: *b* = bottom, *c* = centre, *l* = left, *r* = right, *t* = top

Cover *left* Corbis/Mark Richards/ZUMA; *centre* Corbis; *right* Corbis/Orion Press; Pages 1 Gulf Images; 2–3 Getty/Photonica; 4–5 SaudiAramco World; 7 Getty/NGS; 8*tl* Corbis/K.M.Westermann; 8*cl* Alamy/Israel Images; 9 Getty/Time Life; 10 Getty/Lonely Planet Images; 10–11 Corbis; 10–11*b* Still/Roland Seitre; 11*tr* Getty/Stone; 12 – all left to right: Corbis/Reza; Webistan; Alamy/Danita Delimont; Corbis/Peter Guttman; Corbis/Nik Wheeler; Corbis/Reuters; 13 – all left to right: Getty/Imagebank; Corbis/Gianni Giansanti; Corbis/Reuters; 14*cl* Getty News/David Silverman; 14*bl* Corbis/Paul Almasy; 14–15 Corbis/Kazuyoshi Nomachi; 15*tr* Corbis/Christine Osbourne; 15*br* Getty/AFP; 16*cl* Bridgeman Art Library/Bibliotheque Nationale, Paris, France; 16*tr* Corbis/Bojan Breceli; 18*bl* Corbis/Gianni Dagli Orti; 18–19 The Art Archive/Topkapi Museum Istanbul/Dagli Orti; 19*tr* Getty/Lonely Planet Images; 19*br* Bridgeman Art Library/Forum, Rome; 20*tr* Corbis/Elio Ciol; 20*bl* Mary Evans Picture Library; 21*tc&tr* Kobal; 20–21*b* Corbis/Carl & Ann Purcell; 22–23 Corbis/ Yann Arthus-Bertrand; 22*tr* Getty/Stone; 23*tl* Corbis/Kristi J. Black; 23*tr* Corbis/Martin Harvey; 24*tr* Saudi Aramco World; 24*cl* Corbis/Ed Kashi; 24*br* Alamy; 25*t* Corbis/Scott Gog; 25*b* Getty/Stone; 26*tr* Getty News/Scott Peterson; 26*bl* Getty/AFP; 27*tr* Getty News/Paula Bronstein; 27*b* Corbis/In Visu; 28 The Art Archive/Museum of Carthage/Dagli Orti; 29 Corbis/zefa; 30*bl* Getty/AFP; 30–31 Getty/AFP; 31*t* Corbis/Howard Davies; 31*b* Corbis/Reuters; 32*bl* Corbis/Dave Bartruff; 32–33 Alamy/Ernst Wrba; 33*tr* Getty/AFP; 33*b* Corbis/Jonathan Blair; 34*tl* Getty/Robert Harding; 34*b* Corbis/K.M. Westermann; 35*t* Corbis/Reuters; 35*b* Corbis/Christine Osborne; 36*b* Getty/AFP; 36–37*t* Corbis/Ed Kashi; 37*tr* Alamy/Cephas; 37*b* Alamy/Mike Goldwater; 38*tr* Alamy/Israel Images; 38*bl* Corbis/Tim Page; 38–39*b* Corbis/Gideon Mendel; 39*tr* Corbis/Yonathan Weitzman; 39*br* Alamy/Israel Images; 40*tr* Alamy/Israel Images; 40*b* Getty News/Uriel Sinai; 41*t* Corbis/Richard T. Nowitz; 42*cl* Getty/Frans Lemmens; 42*tr* Alamy/Gary Cook; 43*tr* Getty/Taxi; 43*b* Getty/Stone; 44*tl* Alamy/Stock Image; 44–45 Getty/Stone; 45*tr* Getty/Robert Harding; 45*br* Getty/Imagebank; 46–47 Getty/Stone; 46*tr* Corbis/Reuters; 46*bl* Corbis/Kazuyoshi Nomachi; 47*tr* Corbis/K.M. Westermann; 48*tl* Science Photo Library/Diccon Alexander; 48–49*b* Corbis/Chris Lisle; 49*tr* Corbis/Yann Arthus-Bertrand; 50*tl* Corbis/Jose Fuste Raga; 50*br* Empics/AP; 51*t* Getty/AFP; 51*bl* Getty News/Joe Raedle; 52*tr* Corbis/David Butow; 52*br* Alamy/Images&Stories; 53 Corbis/Reuters; 54*l* Alamy/Tibor Bognor; 43*r* Alamy/Paul Doyle Pics; 55*tr* Corbis/Sygma; 55*b* Corbis/Michael S. Yamashita; 56*tl* Corbis/ Ric Ergenbright; 57*b* Getty News/Paula Bronstein; 57*b* Getty News/Scott Peterson; 58 Getty/Stone; 60*bl* Corbis/Werner Forman; 60–61*t* Corbis/Philadelphia Museum of Art; 61*br* Corbis/Gianni Dagli Orti; 62–63 Corbis; 64 Alamy/Helene Rogers.

The publisher would like to thank the following illustrators:
Julian Baker 8–9, 23, Thomas Bayley 16–17, David Harris 12, Peter Winfield 40, 41, 52, 57